HOW HANU BECAME HANUMAN

Written and illustrated by K G Subramanyan

Seagull Books
CALCUTTA, 2019

First published in 1995 at the Fine Arts Fair
by the Graphic Art Department,
Faculty of Fine Arts, M. S. University of Baroda.

Seagull Books, 1996
Second printing, 2008
Third printing, 2019

ISBN 978 8 17046 135 7

Published by Naveen Kishore
Seagull Books Private Limited
36C, S.P. Mukherjee Road, Calcutta 700 025

Typeset by Seagull Books, Calcutta, India
Printed and bound by Hyam Enterprises, Calcutta, India

Raghu met Hanu in a dense jungle. Hanu was lounging on the branch of a tree and looking at a string of pearls.

That caught Raghu's eye.

'Where did you get that?' he asked Hanu.

Hanu stared at him and said, 'From a low-flying helicopter, with ten ruffians and a girl. She was chopping away at them and this string loosened off from her neck. My bird-friend Jet tried to intercede but he could not stop them. They knocked him out.'

'That's my girl they have run away with!' said Raghu, feeling helpless and furious.

That made Hanu sit up.

'Your girl? That girl with the black belt?'

'Brave one, she! We can't let her come to harm.'

'Can I be of some help?'

'What kind of help?' asked Raghu.

'You watch and see,' said Hanu. 'I can jump from tree to tree, I can float in the air. I can smell and see across a continent. I can shrink to the size of a flea and swell to the size of a cloud. I can crush rocks between my fingers and cross the seas in a leap. Don't, my dear, underestimate your ancestor.'

‘My ancestor?’

‘That is what others say. That apes are the ancestors of human beings. I presume you are a human being. And you can see I am an ape. The apes that got an extra dose of brain grew human. But lost their earlier powers.

So, you see, you can do great things with your mind but I can do some things with my body.’

Raghu found in Hanu a good ally.

Hanu jumped high and saw that the girl was locked up on a remote island. And, imagine, a discotheque! Surrounded by bulging beauties of all kinds. Wheedling her to be like them with plucked eyebrows, blood-red lips, hair made a mess, bodies padded up.

'I know how to handle them,' said Hanu.

He put on his travelling cap. And tousled the hair on his face.

And 'z-o-o-m'—he flew to where they were.

SMOK
DISCO

The girls fled in panic. He smashed the microphones and pulled out the wires.

'Who are you, daddy? asked Raghu's girl and took a stance to fight. Hanu knew how to handle black-belt girls. He knocked her out in a jiffy. And carried her, in a faint, the whole way through.

It was only when he threw her in Raghu's arms did she come to herself. There was no end to their joy. Though how they showed it was not to Hanu's taste. So he pulled down his cap.

Raghu asked Hanu to go with him. 'No, my boy,' said Hanu, 'I can only live on trees. But if you lose any other girl, you can call me up. I'll be glad to help.'

Raghu did not forget Hanu. He had three big posters above his chair in his office. Two were of Superman and Batman, heroes of his childhood. But above them, larger than life, was one of Hanuman, his real-life hero.